Model-Making Mindset

Flying Models

From soaring flight to real rockets

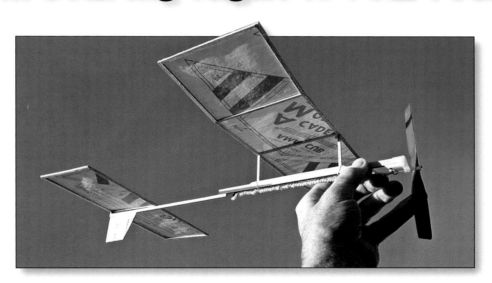

David Jefferis

Crabtree Publishing Company
www.crabtreebooks.com

Introduction

Welcome to *Flying Models*, the book about a hobby and interest with roots that go back to gliding experiments carried out about 200 years ago.

Today, you can make many kinds of flying models. You can enjoy the hobby at home, with friends at school, or with other modelers at a local club.

You need to learn various skills to enjoy flying models. But if you learn them well, the hobby can last for a lifetime.

David Jefferis. Editor: Scale Model News

Special thanks to Séan Galway and Robert MacGregor for their knowledge and guidance.

Crabtree Publishing Company

www.crabtreebooks.com   1-800-387-7650

Written and produced for Crabtree Publishing by:
David Jefferis

Technical advisor:
Mat Irvine FBIS (Fellow of the British Interplanetary Society)

Editor:
Petrice Custance

Prepress Technicians:
Margaret Amy Salter

Proofreader:
Wendy Scavuzzo

Print Coordinator:
Margaret Amy Salter

Printed in the USA/102018/CG20180907

Acknowledgements
We wish to thank all those people who have helped to create this publication and provided images.
Individuals:
Paul Chapman
Mat Irvine
David Jefferis
Keith Laumer
Gavin Page/The Design Shop
Organisations:
Air Hogs
Boeing Phantom Works
Cobra Toys
Fotolia
   Backiris, Black Diamond 67,
   Leung Chopan, Christopher Hall,
   Lalsstock, Serguei Liachenko,
   Photoprofi30, Pichitchai, Terex

Guillow's
Infinite Flight
George Mason University
LHC Leamington Hobby Centre
NASA
Novarossi
Opener.aero
Revell
Scale Model News
Scale Model Scenery
SFO San Francisco Airport
Tuscarora RC Flying Club

The right of David Jefferis to be identified as the Author of this work has been asserted by him in accordance with the Copyrights, Designs and Patents Act 1988.

Library and Archives Canada Cataloguing in Publication

Jefferis, David, author
      Flying models : from soaring flight to real rockets /
David Jefferis.

(Model-making mindset)
Includes index.
Issued in print and electronic formats.
ISBN 978-0-7787-5015-4 (hardcover).--
ISBN 978-0-7787-5019-2 (softcover).--
ISBN 978-1-4271-2133-2 (HTML)

      1. Flying-machines--Models--Juvenile literature. 2. Models and modelmaking--Juvenile literature. I. Title.

TL770.J44 2018   j796.15'4   C2018-903057-7
                                               C2018-903058-5

Library of Congress Cataloging-in-Publication Data

Names: Jefferis, David, author.
Title: Flying models : from soaring flight to real rockets / David Jefferis.
Description: New York, NY : Crabtree Publishing, [2019] |
  Series: Model-making mindset | Includes index.
Identifiers: LCCN 2018042055 (print) | LCCN 2018042380 (ebook) |
  ISBN 9781427121332 (Electronic) |
  ISBN 9780778750154 (hardcover : alk. paper) |
  ISBN 9780778750192 (pbk. : alk. paper)
Subjects: LCSH: Airplanes--Models--Juvenile literature. | Rockets
  (Aeronautics)--Models--Juvenile literature.
Classification: LCC TL770 (ebook) | LCC TL770 .J44 2019 (print) |
  DDC 629.133/1--dc23
LC record available at https://lccn.loc.gov/2018042055

Contents

What is a flying model?

Flying models include a wide range of aircraft that you can build. The cheapest and easiest of all is the dart, which you can make by simply folding a sheet of paper (above). It glides through the air after you throw it, and is known as a "chuck" glider.

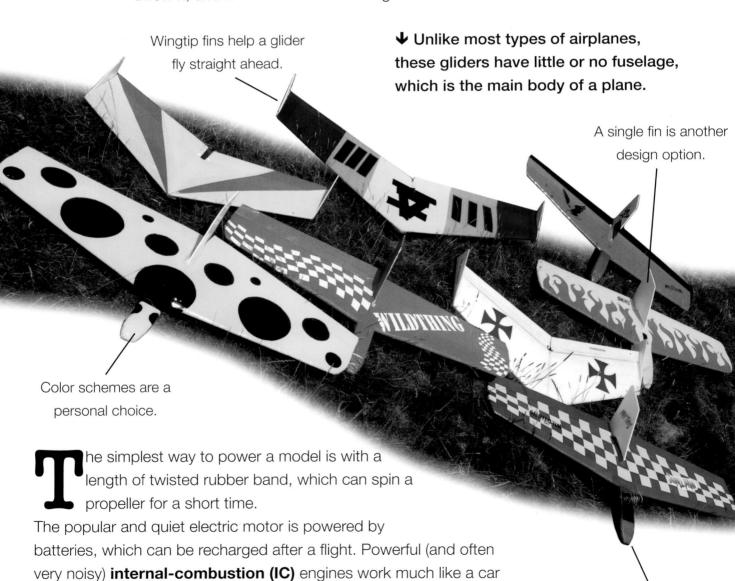

Wingtip fins help a glider fly straight ahead.

↓ Unlike most types of airplanes, these gliders have little or no fuselage, which is the main body of a plane.

A single fin is another design option.

Color schemes are a personal choice.

Extra length may give extra stability in flight.

The simplest way to power a model is with a length of twisted rubber band, which can spin a propeller for a short time. The popular and quiet electric motor is powered by batteries, which can be recharged after a flight. Powerful (and often very noisy) **internal-combustion (IC)** engines work much like a car or motorcycle engine. They can run on various fuels, such as glow fuel, which is a mixture of **methanol**, **nitromethane**, and oil.

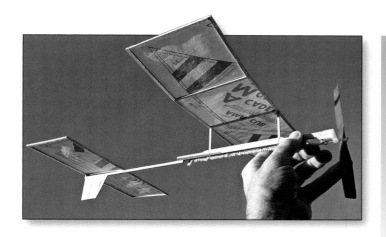

↑ This rubber-band-powered model has a featherlight construction. The wings are covered with a super-thin plastic covering.

5 •

✈ Why build planes?

First of all, it's fun! Taking a model out for its first test flight can be thrilling. You also learn valuable skills while building flying models, such as how to apply the basic principles of flight or how to use new tools correctly. Remember that different areas have different rules for flying models. For a full list of rules, please visit www.modelaircraft.org in the U.S., and http://maac.ca in Canada.

↑ This model is based on a P-39 fighter, used in **World War II**. It is powered by an electric motor, which is rechargeable between flights.

↑ Drones are guided from a handset, and many have video cameras. You can see the drone camera's view using an app.

Flying models come in three basic types. Free-flight (FF) models fly on their own after launch. Control-line (CL) models fly in circles, held by a thin cable, with movements adjusted by your hand. Radio-control (RC) models have radio equipment on board. This adjusts the flight controls from commands you send, using a handset similar to the one at right.

→ There are many types of RC handsets, but they all perform a similar function. They all control a flying model from the ground.

Fliers big and small

Whatever their size or shape, flying models come in three main forms: **scale**, semi-scale, and non-scale. Scale flying models aim to look as much like real aircraft as possible. Semi-scale models may look fairly realistic, but flying qualities are more important than being an exact replica. Non-scale models are built purely for flight, and can look like anything the designer wants.

Semi-scale RC model is based on a full-size Yak-54. Both are built for **aerobatic** competitions.

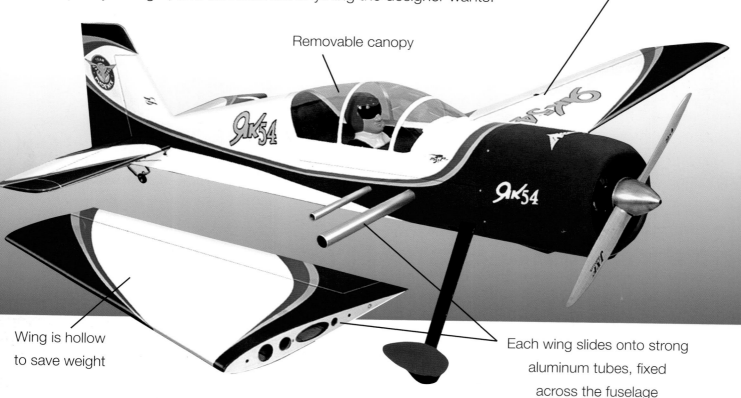

Removable canopy

Wing is hollow to save weight

Each wing slides onto strong aluminum tubes, fixed across the fuselage

Flying models offer much more than out-of-the-box fun, because there is a lot to learn as you build. There's a near-endless range of choice, which provides aeromodelers with assorted levels of interest, skill, and control.

These include learning something about **aerodynamics**, electronics, mechanics, **drafting**, and design. Knowledge of construction, and of different materials is also important.

↑ The wings of this large model detach easily. This makes it easier to pack it for trips to flying areas.

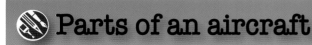

Parts of an aircraft

The language of flying models uses terms from the full-size world of aviation. The fin, rudder, and elevator section is also called the tail assembly or empennage.

Drones and helicopters have their own terms, such as the main rotors that lift them off the ground. A helicopter may also have a tail rotor to help control its direction of flight.

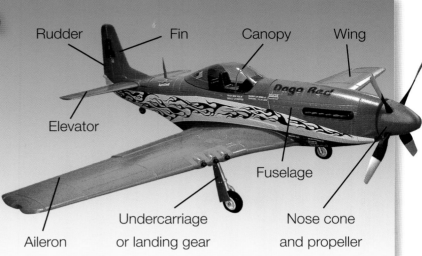

Rudder   Fin   Canopy   Wing

Elevator

Fuselage

Aileron   Undercarriage or landing gear   Nose cone and propeller

Reading a set of plans correctly is a core skill when it comes to making a flying model. The reduced-size plan (right) includes drawn outlines of the wing and fuselage, plus many useful notes and instructions.

➔ **The plan also shows how to paint the finished airplane, an important part of making a good-looking flying model.**

Engine molding   Scale pilot figure

The 1930s-era Gee Bee Model Z (right) is a 1:10 scale model, meaning that it is ten times smaller than the real thing. The engine is a realistic **molding**, for the Gee Bee has an electric motor inside.

Ready-to-fly or build your own?

Flying modelers have plenty of kits to choose from stores and internet suppliers. There are thousands of flying models, and you can get one to suit your budget and skill level. The easiest could be a ready-to-fly (RTF) model. With RTFs, there is little or no assembly involved. The skills are with setup and flight.

↑ Both these airplanes were designed as ARTF models. The RC fighter plane (right) has **retractable** landing gear.

The next level up is an almost-ready-to-fly (ARTF) kit. Here, some parts do need to be assembled, but usually only a few minutes of careful work is involved.

Once the airplane has been put together, the next step is to choose a calm day for your first flight. Gusty winds are the enemy, as they make it easy for a learner pilot to lose control.

The forces of flight

All aircraft juggle four forces, each of which has an opposite force that works against it.

Moving forward allows the wings to generate upward thrust called lift (1). When enough lift is generated, an airplane can overcome its weight (2) and leave the ground.

Thrust (3) is usually provided by an engine of some sort. This provides forward motion, and overcomes **drag** (4).

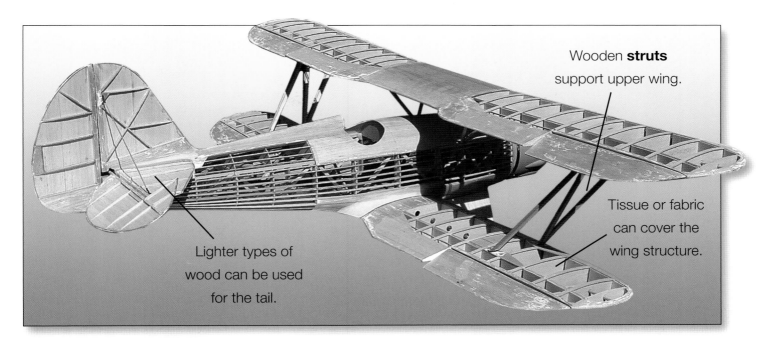

Wooden **struts** support upper wing.

Lighter types of wood can be used for the tail.

Tissue or fabric can cover the wing structure.

↑ This partly built Waco YMF is a biplane, or an aircraft with two sets of wings, one above the other. It is too difficult for a beginner to make, but it could be a future project.

Beyond starter kits, flying models are more of a challenge. Basic materials are often an assorted mixture, including molded plastics and **balsa** wood. Balsa is a lightweight wood that has been used for making flying models since the dawn of the hobby, more than a century ago.

When assembled and glued together as a close-fitting framework, balsa becomes a light but strong material. You can put together the various parts in groups, ready for final assembly when they have all been finished.

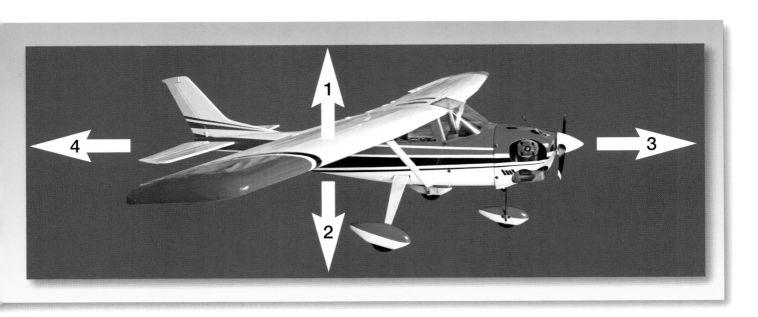

Planning your model air base

Allow room for parts to spread as you assemble your model.

Numbered components let you follow instructions easily.

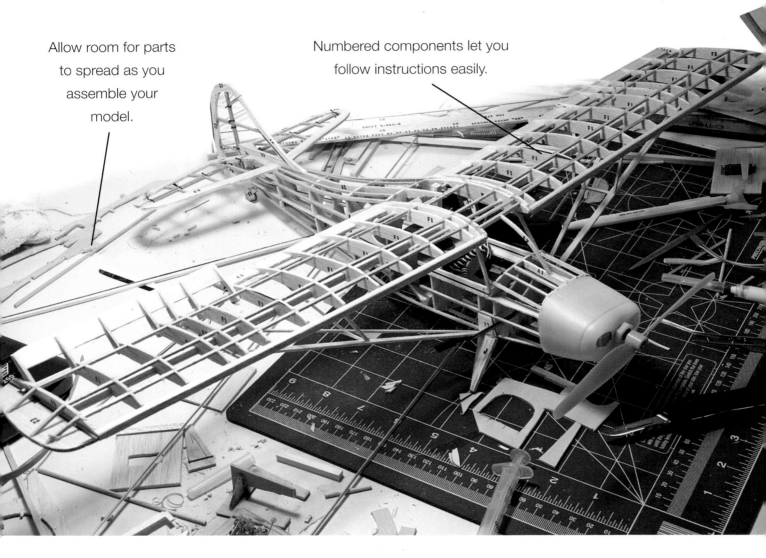

Having a comfortable space to build a flying model can be difficult to achieve. The best idea is to use your own room or a den. But many modelers may have to work in a living room corner, perhaps putting their flight gear away when other people need to use the space.

Whether you have a big or small modeling area, you will have to plan how to use that space as well as possible.

↑ **This partly built aircraft shows that plenty of work space is essential, not only for the model itself, but also for the various tools needed.**

↑ Balsa wood is an important construction material. You could store different sizes and shapes in a corner of your air base.

↑ Foam plastic is a lightweight material, used here for a biplane fighter. It's easy to fly, but your air base will be needed for any repairs.

If you are lucky, you may have room for a work bench that's nicely tucked away from interruptions. If so, you'll be able to leave models, tools, and components in place after a modeling session. It's an ideal solution, because you can leave a flight project in mid-build, then carry on with it later on.

Shelves and drawers provide useful storage for paints, brushes, tools, and accessories. Good lighting is essential for model making, especially for close work, and make sure that you do not work in shadow.

↓ Proper storage becomes essential as your collection of tools grows. The brushes, paints, and glues shown here are just the beginning.

🖌 Avoid fumes

Using model glues and paints can be a smelly business. So the healthy plan is to avoid breathing in any fumes they may give off.

Be sure to make flying models only where there is good **ventilation**, which will allow you to breathe clean air.

A good idea is to have your workspace near a window, always keeping it open a little while you work.

Assembly skills

To construct a flying model successfully, you will need the grit and determination to learn the many skills required. First, there's reading and understanding the supplied instructions. Second, there's cutting and shaping the various parts accurately. That's followed by cementing the parts together, and covering the flight surface neatly in a thin plastic covering.

There's also radio control equipment, engines, and fuel systems to learn about. If all that sounds like a lot to cover before you start flying, you're right. But building a model that flies well is hugely satisfying—so it's all worth it!

↓ Your hard work can result in flying models such as these, nicely assembled and ready for their first flight.

Both airplanes are highly aerobatic, with powerful engines for flying in competitions

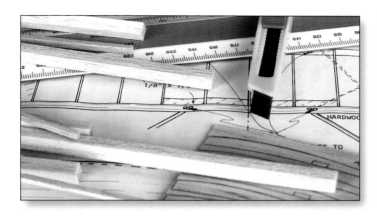

↑ Make sure you check your shaped parts against the instructions, so you don't make a mistake and have to start again.

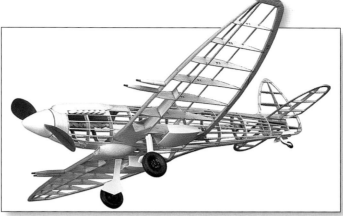

↑ During building, this balsa fighter kit looks like a wooden skeleton. It will be transformed when the plastic covering is added.

One important rule for any model-making job is to never rush it. Concentration and patience are among the keys to creating any miniature, and that certainly includes flying models such as those in this book.

Unlike models made for display, flying models are rough-and-tumble machines that may (and most likely will) have many high-speed crashes, or flights that end up in trees or bushes.

So, taking the time to construct a strongly built airplane that can handle plenty of damage will be well worth the effort.

↑ This electric motor is ready to power a flying model.

↑ Closeup of a custom drone, being built from various parts, rather than from a kit.

Electronics in the air

Assembling and checking electronics and wiring is an important part of making a powered flying model. If you build from a kit, then it's usually a matter of carefully following the instructions provided in the box.

But it's also possible to buy many of the components separately, giving you a chance to design your own flight-ready model.

Silent flight

Gliders are the oldest type of airplanes, dating back to the early 1800s. Today, model gliders range from ultra-simple chuck designs to larger radio-controlled models. These are usually launched by hand, either from underneath, as though throwing a dart, or sometimes from the wingtip using a flicking motion.

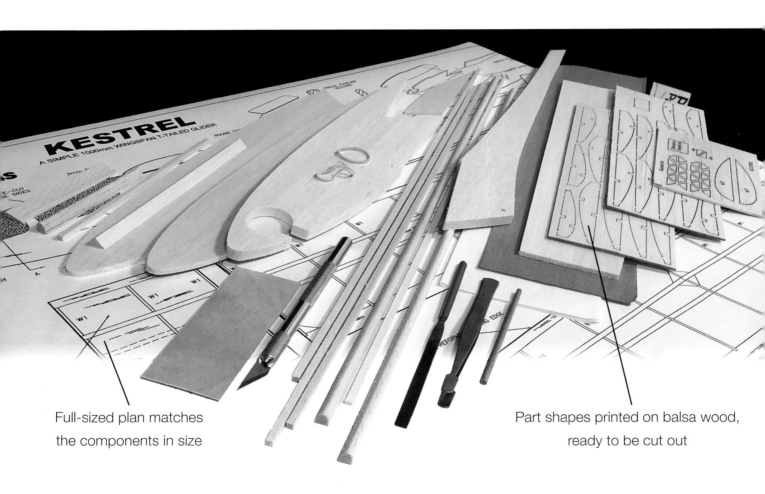

Full-sized plan matches the components in size

Part shapes printed on balsa wood, ready to be cut out

The glider kit (above) assembles to make a free-flight model. For a flight, you have to set the controls so that after launch, the glider will fly in a straight line. With other adjustments, it may circle round to land near your launch site.

More advanced gliders can use rising air currents to gain height. And by using a radio control system, a skilled pilot can keep a glider in the air for hours at a time.

↑ **A starter glider kit allows you to practice construction skills, such as accurately cutting out parts and joining them together.**

↑ This simple chuck glider has a design based on the swept-wing Avro Arrow, a fast Canadian jet that flew in the late 1950s.

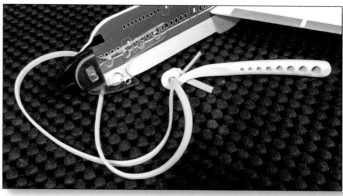

↑ A step up from throwing a chuck glider is to use a rubber-band launcher, which sends the glider into the air at high speed.

Many model gliders are made mostly of balsa wood, with tissue-covered wings. Pre-shaped foam plastic is also a very popular material, and can allow you to assemble a model very quickly.

But whatever the glider is made of, weight is a vital issue. With no engine—and especially if carrying the weight of RC equipment—a glider needs to be as light as possible.

With radio control, and plenty of skill, you can send your glider soaring along a hilly ridge, supported by air that flows up the sides. Or you can circle tightly to gain height, inside a rising column of air.

🛩 Motions in flight

During a flight, an airplane moves in three directions—up, down, and side to side. A pilot uses the flight controls to change the flight angle, in one of three ways:

Pitch: Elevators on the tail move up or down, allowing the airplane to climb or dive.

Roll—The ailerons on the edge of each wing move to tilt the plane from side to side.

Yaw—The rudder is attached to the rear of the tail fin. Its movement helps adjust the plane's direction.

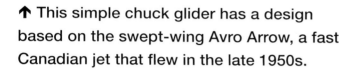

→ RC soaring along a cliff top is not for beginners. But an experienced pilot could fly here without difficulty.

Rubber power

The oldest form of powered flight is a propeller spinning from the energy contained in an unwinding rubber band. There have been few big changes over the years, though modern rubber bands are more efficient than older types, and give longer flight times.

The Chipmunk trainer is a typical starter rubber-band-powered model. Its single rubber band runs inside the fuselage.

Advanced modelers may use several very long rubber bands, which are used together. To prepare for a flight, you wind up the multi-strand rubber band, sometimes hundreds of times. Overwinding is a danger, as the band may snap,

↑ Like many balsa kits, this Chipmunk has some extra plastic parts, here including the nose cone, propeller, and cockpit canopy.

perhaps damaging the aircraft as it does so. To avoid this, you can use an electronic counter, which keeps track of the number of turns you have given the band.

Rubber band stretches behind the propeller

↑ **This free-flight rubber-band-powered Mustang is a semi-scale model. It looks much like a real plane, but is not an exact scale replica.**

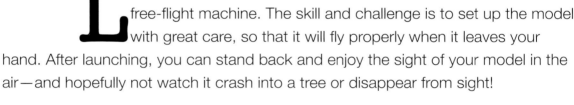

Like a simple glider, a typical rubber-band-powered aircraft is a free-flight machine. The skill and challenge is to set up the model with great care, so that it will fly properly when it leaves your hand. After launching, you can stand back and enjoy the sight of your model in the air—and hopefully not watch it crash into a tree or disappear from sight!

↑ **The paddle-like propeller was at the tail, which pushed the model forward.**

The first flier

The earliest rubber-band-powered model airplane was perfected in 1871, by the Frenchman Alphonse Pénaud (1850–1880).

He called his model (left) the Planophore, which had another advanced feature as well as its twisted-rubber "engine." The model was very stable in flight, made possible by using upturned wingtips. The Planophore had a wingspan of just 18 inches (46 cm).

Airborne engines

Traditionally, powered flying models always had internal-combustion (IC) engines, miniature versions of those we use in automobiles or motorcycles. Today, electric motors are widely available, but powerful IC engines still have an important place in the flying model world.

Muffler reduces engine noise

Radiator fins help release engine heat

Engine screwed tightly to the front of the fuselage

Pipe from fuel tank to engine

Two-bladed propeller

There are various types of IC engines, and they still have some advantages over electric power. These include more weight, which often allows smoother flying in gusty winds. Bigger IC engines also provide sheer power, which is needed for very large model aircraft, perhaps up to 1:4 or 1:3 scale.

↑ **This aircraft looks clean, but the photo was taken before flight. After a day's flying, oily exhaust streaks will need cleaning off.**

Taking photos of flying models

You don't need an expensive camera to take great photos. Most cell phones come with a camera good enough to take a picture similar to the one above.

A steady hand and a sunny day will help you get the best results. However, if you want to take pictures of your model while it's flying, you will need a camera with a zoom lens to capture an action shot. Even the best cell phone would likely only show a tiny blob in the middle of a large expanse of sky.

Using an IC engine involves plenty of challenges. Among them are strict regulations, which may mean you can often fly only from a recognized model club flying field. Noise is an issue, too, since local residents may not like the loud sound of an IC engine. But those kinds of problems aside, meeting other flying model fans to learn the skills involved makes it a hugely enjoyable and satisfying hobby.

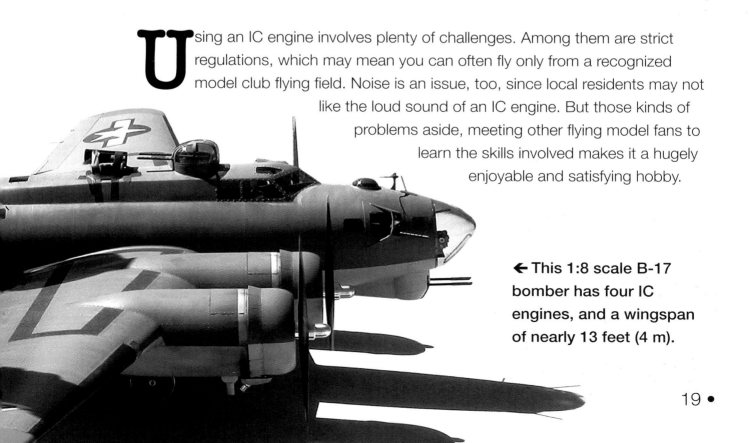

← This 1:8 scale B-17 bomber has four IC engines, and a wingspan of nearly 13 feet (4 m).

Electric motors

Electricity is now the most popular way to power a flying model. Using electricity offers several advantages—it's quiet, clean, and by using rechargeable batteries, the cost per flight is very low.

↑ The jet-like RC Avanti has an EDF motor buried inside the fuselage.

Most electric flying models use a propeller in the front. But if you want to model a jet aircraft, you need to get rid of that old-fashioned propeller. The answer is an electric ducted fan (EDF) motor. Here, the propeller is enclosed by a tube, which directs the airflow at high speed out of the back. You can bury an EDF inside a model, and it looks just like a jet plane.

Motor

Wires connecting motor to battery

← The EDF is a simple design that shrinks a propeller to the size of a small fan. Air is sucked in by the fan, then blown out of the aircraft's tail to push the plane forward.

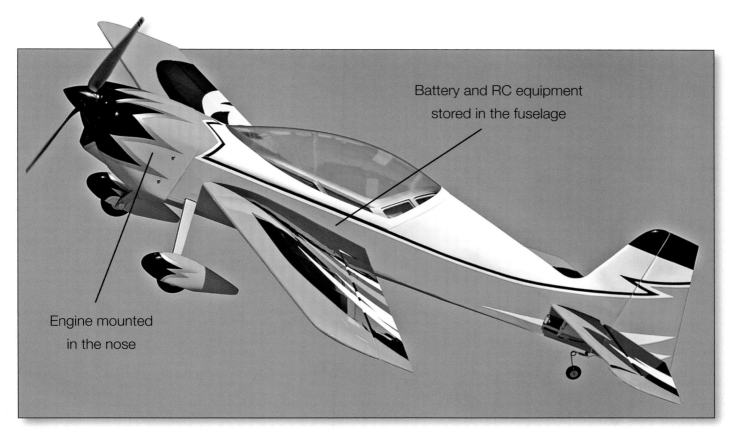

Battery and RC equipment stored in the fuselage

Engine mounted in the nose

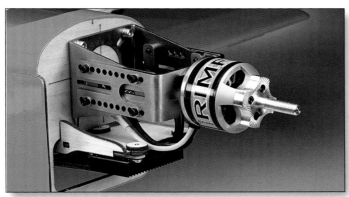

← ↑ An electric motor is usually mounted in a propeller plane's nose. The RC equipment and battery are carried farther back, in the fuselage. This keeps the aircraft in balance, which is essential because a nose-heavy machine usually flies straight into the ground.

Electric motors have two big advantages over IC engines. They are clean, and they are quiet, making them good to work with, and much better for non-flying neighbors who may dislike unwanted noise.

But sound is also part of the fun with electric flying models. Some companies now use digital sound, which can **simulate**, for example, the growling roar of a powerful World War II-era fighter engine.

 Watch your fingers

Spinning propellers are a danger with all powered flying models. Always use caution when flying your model. Keep your hands and fingers away from the propeller. Only fly your model in clear weather, and always be sure to keep a safe distance from trees and buildings.

Model helicopters

Rotors, or rotating wings, are the secret to a helicopter's ability to take off and land almost anywhere. Unlike an aircraft with wings, you don't need a large flying area for a helicopter. Instead, a backyard can serve as your own airport.

Rotors spin in opposite directions, to stop the helicopter from spinning in circles.

Light plastic molding covers the nose.

← A small electric helicopter such as this is good to practice with, though it's best flown indoors.

↑ IC engine helicopters can fly longer than electric machines. However, they create noise and pollution, which are serious drawbacks.

Practice and patience are the keys to becoming a model helicopter pilot. Flying one successfully means learning a delicate balancing act between the various controls, and it takes time to operate these well.

But the smallest model helicopters are electric-powered, which makes practice much easier than with larger machines with IC engines.

Electric helicopters are clean and quiet, and the smallest ones can fly indoors. This means that it's possible to fly after sunset, or when there's bad weather.

The best way to transport a model helicopter is in a metal case, such as the one above. Photographers use similar cases for delicate camera equipment. Cases have padded foam cushions inside for protection against bumps and knocks.

The case also acts as a handy takeoff platform, especially useful here, as it enables the helicopter's rotors to spin freely, clear of long grass at the launch point.

↑ When ready for takeoff, stand well back, in case a gust of wind blows the helicopter toward you.

Is there any danger?

The short answer is yes. Spinning rotor blades, especially those of a powerful IC machine, can easily damage anything they hit.

The answer is to fly only in open areas, and keep away from anything that looks as though you might contact it.

Small helicopters are less of an issue, but the rotor blades are delicate and will break if they hit something solid, even a hedge.

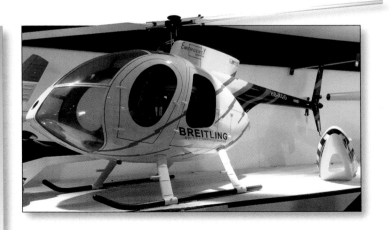

↑ Big models can fetch big money. This 1:10 scale Hughes 500 is priced at more than $1,000—and that's for a used machine!

Drones at your command

rones are a type of helicopter, with four or more rotors and miniaturized onboard computers that control stability in flight. This means you avoid the learning curve of flying a single-rotor helicopter, and can start flight operations the moment your drone's batteries are fully charged.

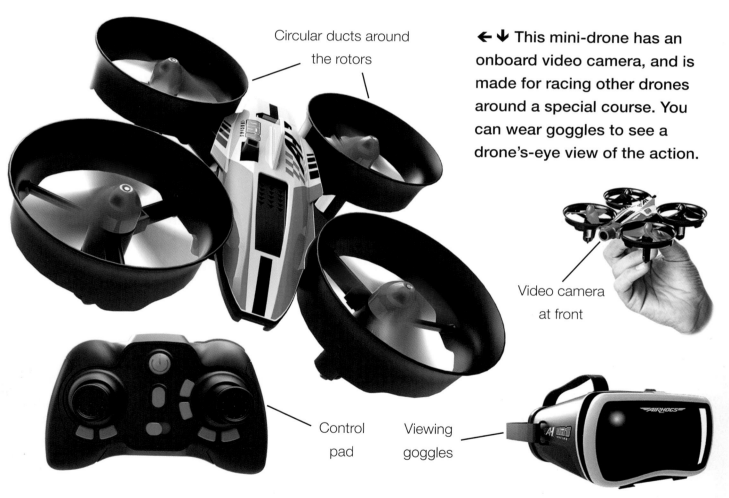

Circular ducts around the rotors

← ↓ This mini-drone has an onboard video camera, and is made for racing other drones around a special course. You can wear goggles to see a drone's-eye view of the action.

Video camera at front

Control pad

Viewing goggles

ulti-rotor drones take off, hover, and steer by using different amounts of power sent to each rotor. You control a drone by using a handset, much like those used for other RC fliers. Like other flying models, the smallest drones are really suitable only for flying indoors, or in very calm weather outside.

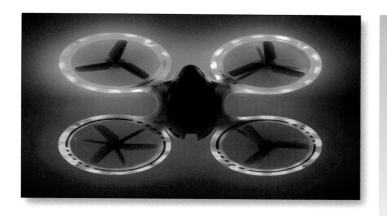

↑ Some drones have **LED** lights, which allow flying after dark. However, some places ban night flights for drones, so check before flying.

Bigger and more expensive drones can fly high and far, and even can carry top-quality cameras. However, high-end machinery is expensive, so it's no surprise that these drones are used only by professionals, often to help with the production of film and TV shows, or for music videos. And of course, drones are important tools that are used widely for general photography and survey work.

↓ The plastic body has been removed to show the electronics inside a quadcopter, or four-rotor, drone. Other drones may have five or more rotors.

Rocket launch

Model rocketry is a sky-high flying hobby. The Estes company offers a large range of model rockets. You can start with a simple RTF rocket, then work your way up to complex machinery that looks as though it might be flown by the NASA space agency.

← **At takeoff, a rocket slides up a thick wire, which keeps it stable for the first moments of flight.**

↓ **A typical kit includes the rocket and its launch pad. Connectors and a push-button launch control pad are often included.**

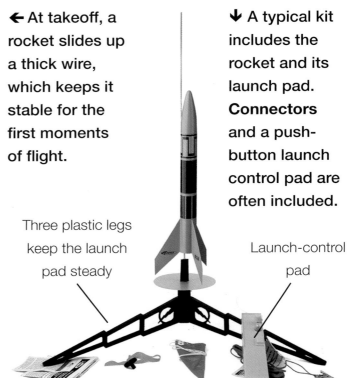

Three plastic legs keep the launch pad steady

Launch-control pad

Model rockets should be launched outside in an area that is free of power lines and trees, and well away from buildings. For safety, an adult should be present to help you launch your rocket. For a full set of safety guidelines, visit www.nar.org/safety-information/model-rocket-safety-code.

↑ Some rockets are designed to glide for long distances after they have run out of fuel. There are competitions for rocket-gliders.

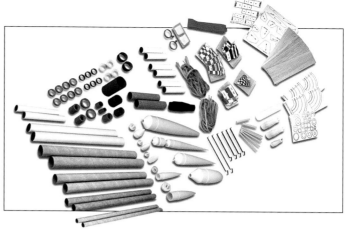

↑ Many parts are available to allow you to create and build your own rocket designs. The parts here are all from one big kit.

↑ A water rocket, ready to launch from a homemade launch pad. The yellow tire pump is ready to clip on to the rocket's nozzle.

For a bit of fun, you can also try flying a water rocket. A kit normally includes a nozzle with a set of fins, ready to attach to the neck of a used plastic soda bottle. You clip a bicycle tire pump to the nozzle, then pump up the bottle with air.

Moments later, the trapped air in the bottle pushes the water out of the nozzle, and with a massive squirt, the rocket flies high into the air.

Recovery by parachute – or maybe not!

The curse of many rocketeers is a strong wind that carries your rocket off course, and may make recovery impossible.

The only real solution is to choose a calm day for flying, and even then, there may be gusty winds above ground level.

You can help yourself by choosing a launch site with no nearby power lines or cables (right) to prevent trouble-free landings.

What's next?

The X-48B is a small version of a huge design. If built, the full-size machine would have a wingspan of 240 feet (73 m).

The X-48B has been test-flown with the NASA space agency, at one of its bases in California.

Making scale models is not just for hobbyists. Even in today's computer-aided design world, there are plenty of times when a real-life flying model is needed. One of these is the Boeing X-48B (above) which was built to prove that an unusual new design could fly safely. Power comes from three small jet engines at the rear. The 21-foot (6.4-m) wingspan machine flies under RC command from a ground operator.

↑ **The X-48B could fly for up to 40 minutes at a time.**

➔ **If the weather is bad, you can still go flying—indoors with a computer flight simulator app. This picture shows a screen shot from the realistic Infinite Flight app.**

↑ The BlackFly single-seat electric airplane was designed in Warkworth, Canada. Flights are controlled by eight drone-type propellers.

↑ You could start creating new designs, such as this UFO-like drone. You could even find a job in the modeling or aerospace industries.

The worlds of flying models, conventional airplanes, and drone technology are coming together. Drones are now so reliable that they can be scaled up to make larger, "people-sized" machines. Learning to fly may also become easier and cheaper. For example, the Canadian Opener company says you might need only a few minutes of training to fly its all-electric BlackFly safely.

Even so, learning to make and fly models will continue to be a fascinating and challenging hobby, and the skills of designing and building will always be useful.

Join forces to find good flying sites

Working with flying models at a local club can be hugely enjoyable, and is of course a great way to take your hobby forward.

A club is also where you can get feedback from fellow modelers on how to improve your skills. A club will almost certainly have a member who has the knowledge you might need to get your model into the air successfully.

You should look for advice on model building and flying, and get easy access to a well-planned flight area.

Glossary

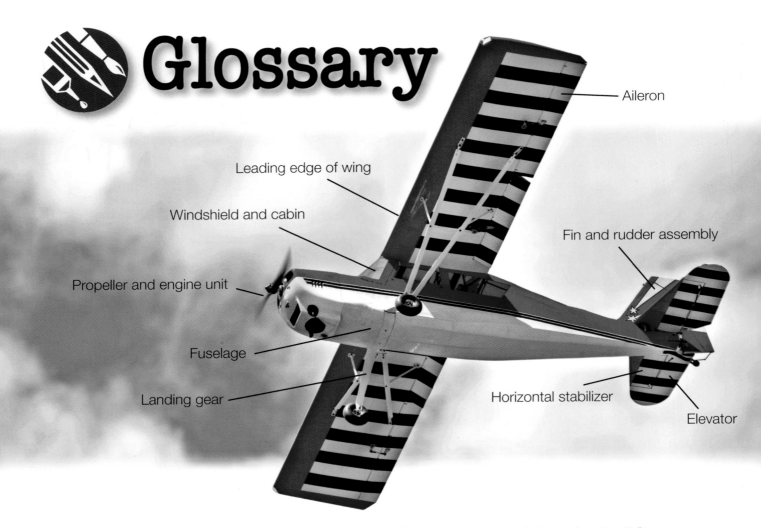

Aileron

Leading edge of wing

Windshield and cabin

Fin and rudder assembly

Propeller and engine unit

Fuselage

Landing gear

Horizontal stabilizer

Elevator

↑ **This flying model carries its RC equipment inside the cabin.**

aerobatic Describing something that does air stunts such as loops, rolls, and spins

aerodynamics The study of motion in air, especially how easily aircraft move through air

balsa The lightweight wood widely used for constructing flying models

connectors Device for joining electrical circuits together

drafting To convert the designs of engineers and architects into technical drawings

drag A force that slows the movement of an object through a liquid or gas

exhaust The gas or vapor given off by a running engine

internal-combustion (IC) An engine that burns fuel in a combustion chamber

LED Short for light emitting diode. In flying models, battery-powered LEDs are lightweight, and offer little or no risk of fire, compared to much hotter traditional light bulbs.

methanol A flammable liquid, one of several fuels used in model IC engines

molding Something formed by liquid plastic poured into a cavity in order to harden into a particular shape

nitromethane Also called nitro, a substance that dissolves other substances, often used in rocket fuel

retractable Able to be drawn back in

scale The amount by which a model is smaller than the real thing

simulate To make something seem like something else

struts Long, thin pieces of wood or metal used for support

ventilation The circulation of air throughout a space

World War II A war between several world nations, lasting from 1939 to 1945

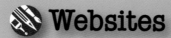

Websites

There are plenty of flying model sites on the Internet, depending on your particular interest. Here are some that should be useful to you.

https://modelaircraft.org
Academy of Model Aeronautics. Annual membership includes insurance, which is a must-have for serious model flying.

www.airhogs.com
Manufacturer of easy-to-fly drones. The range goes from micro-racers to *Star Wars*.

www.canadianfederationfordroneracing.com
The CFDR is a voice for all forms of drone flying, safety being a prime interest. The CFDR's motto is "By the Pilots, For the Pilots."

www.dji.com/flying tips
Home of DJI, a drone manufacturer. DJI is concerned for safety, and this tips page has guidance for drone pilots in many countries.

www.estesrockets.com
Internet home of the biggest model rocket maker. Also offers model planes and drones.

www.horizonhobby.com
Caters to most interests, including drones, planes, helicopters, RC, and much more.

www.nar.org
The National Association of Rocketry is dedicated to education, safety, and the advancement of technology for model rockets.

www.scalemodelnews.com
Short articles on a variety of subjects, also featuring more detailed reviews of new kits. Strong on aerospace, cars, and sci-fi.

 Index

About the author

David Jefferis writes books on science and technology, more than 40 of them produced for Crabtree Publishing.

He also creates features for Scale Model News, a website with readers around the world. For the Model-Making Mindset, David worked closely with Mat Irvine, who makes models for many TV shows. These include *Doctor Who*, the popular BBC sci-fi series.